CAMP
*&*
AND
COTTAGE

# NATURE NOTEBOOK

NORTHWORD
PRESS, INC.

Minocqua, Wisconsin

Illustrations © 1995 Laurie Anderson Caple
Cover design by Amy Monday
Book design by Lisa Moore

Published by
NorthWord Press, Inc.
P.O. Box 1360
Minocqua, WI 54548

For a free catalog describing NorthWord's line of nature books and gift items, call toll free 1-800-336-5666

ISBN 1-55971-469-7

Printed in Canada

*Sweet berries ripen in the wilderness.*

Wallace Stevens

*We shall not cease from exploration*
*And the end of all our exploring*
*Will be to arrive where we started*
*And know the place for the first time.*

*T. S. Eliot*

*N*ature doesn't plan events; nature is the events. The sun and rain, the winds and snows and all the other conditions that prove a hardship for some will benefit others.

Stephen J. Krasemann

*Sometime in April, when light returns and the sun radiates warmth, there commences a time of promise for the year ahead, a time of welcoming all the ambiance of new life into myself.*

Stephen J. Krasemann

*Do not thus drift away with the mob while the spirits of these rocks and waters hail you after long waiting as their kinsman and persuade you to closer communion . . .*

*John Muir*

*What is life? It is the flash of a firefly in the night. It is the breath of a buffalo in the winter time. It is the little shadow which runs across the grass and loses itself in the sunset.*

Crowfoot of the Blackfoot Nation

*To insure health, a man's relation to Nature must*
*come very near to a personal one;*
*he must be conscious of a friendliness in her . . .*

Henry David Thoreau

*I* only went out for a walk, and finally concluded to stay out till sundown, for going out, I found, was really going in.

*John Muir*

*Flowers are words*
*Which even a babe may understand.*

Bishop Coxe

*Let us probe the silent places, let us seek what luck betide us;*
*Let us journey to a lonely land I know.*
*There's a whisper on the night-wind, there's a star agleam to*
*    guide us,*
*        And the Wild is calling, calling . . . let us go.*

Robert Service

*Man must go back to nature for information.*
Thomas Paine

*Is a wolfless north woods any north woods at all?*
Aldo Leopold

*Whether it be a wide unspoiled landscape that inspires us, or the beauty of the humble little wildflower at our feet, the fact remains that we need inspiration to go forward.*

Olaus Murie

*Put your ear close to the whispering branch*
*and you may catch what it is saying.*

Guy Murchie

*Earth laughs in flowers.*

Ralph Waldo Emerson

*Every moment Nature starts on the longest journey,
and every moment she reaches her goal.*

J. W. Von Goethe

*There is no other door to knowledge than the door Nature opens; and there is no truth except the truths we discover in Nature.*

Luther Burbank

. . . to find the universal elements enough;
to find the air and the water exhilarating;
to be refreshed by a morning walk or an
evening saunter . . . to be thrilled by the
stars at night; to be elated over a bird's
nest or a wild flower in spring—these are
some of the rewards of the simple life.

John Burroughs

*Earth's crammed with Heaven,*
*And every common bush afire with God.*

Elizabeth Barrett Browning

*To create a little flower is the labour of ages.*
    William Blake

*Forget not that the earth delights to feel your bare feet and the winds long to play with your hair.*
Kahlil Gibran

*Sit outside at midnight and close your eyes; feel the grass, the air, the space. Listen to birds for ten minutes at dawn. Memorize a flower.*

Linda Hasselstrom

*Everything in nature invites us constantly to be what we are. We are often like rivers: careless and forceful, timid and dangerous, lucid and muddied, eddying, gleaming, still.*

Gretel Ehrlich

*To me a lush carpet of pine needles
or spongy grass is more welcome
than the most luxurious Persian rug.*

Helen Keller

*The green earth sends her incense up*
*From many a mountain shrine;*
*From folded leaf and dewey cup*
*She pours her sacred wine.*

John Greenleaf Whittier

*If we have powers of imagination,
these are activated by the magic
display of color and sound, of form
and movement, such as we observe
in the clouds of the sky, the trees
and bushes and flowers, the
waters and the wind, the
singing birds, and the
movement of the great blue
whale through the sea.*

Thomas Berry

*Nature is man's teacher. She unfolds her treasures to his search, unseals his eye, illumes his mind, and purifies his heart; an influence breathes from all the sights and sounds of her existence.*

Alfred Billings Street

*Tonight, during this short trip, the conditions combine to create a mood, a memory of canoe country. Even if we lose the details to time, we'll remember the essence.*

Stephen J. Krasemann

*One touch of nature makes the whole world kin.*

*Shakespeare*

*Is not the sky a father and the earth a mother and are not all living things with feet or wings or roots their children?*

Black Elk

*So where is north now? . . . Ask anyone who loves the north. They will speak of smoky gold tamaracks on sunny October days, bold granite outcrops erupting from pristine blue lakes, a moose swimming across a quiet bay at sunset, or of a stand of white pines old enough to remember the chansons of the voyageurs.*

Tom Klein

*Bathed in endless light, with new leaves sparkling on the birches, the lakes melting and rapidly rising, geese and loons and ducks passing north, a batch of tiny, fast mosquitoes on the wing, the earth drinks up hour after hour, day after day of cool bright sunlight.*

Dave Olsen

*The Lord did well when he put the loon and his music into this lonesome land.*

Aldo Leopold

*One can sit atop a mountain and contemplate an entire region; in the canoe country one sits only on small lichen-covered knobs, surveying intimate scenes. But it is exactly this shyness that is the canoe country's charm and one must probe it slowly and over long years before knowing many of its secrets, before sensing its grandeur.*

Michael Furtman

*Patience is power;
with time and patience the mulberry leaf becomes silk.*
    *Chinese proverb*

*Adventure is not outside a man; it is within.*
David Grayson

*The earth, that is sufficient,*
*I do not want the constellations any nearer,*
*I know they are very well where they are,*
*I know they suffice for those who belong to them.*

*Walt Whitman*

*There is enough for all. The earth is a generous mother; she will provide in plentiful abundance food for all her children if they will but cultivate her soil in justice and in peace.*

Bourke Cockran

*Man must go back to nature for information.*
*Thomas Paine*

*Sit in reverie and watch the changing color of the waves that break upon the idle seashore of the mind.*

Henry Wadsworth Longfellow

*I* never found a companion that was
so companionable as solitude.

Henry David Thoreau

*Sunshine is delicious, rain is refreshing, wind braces up, snow is exhilarating; there is no such thing as bad weather, only different kinds of good weather.*

John Ruskin

*For the strength of the Pack is the Wolf, and the strength of the Wolf is the Pack.*

Rudyard Kipling

*It takes an eagle to bring us down to size.
Though only a fraction of our weight, these birds
dwarf us; for by soaring into the sky, they give
a tangible, vertical dimension to the
observable world.*

Candace Savage

*Campfires are those crackling tongues of flame that begin to murmur as darkness creeps out of the trees. Their wispy curls of smoke hang in the air, as if reluctant to leave the pale flames, the orange, glowing coals, and the occasional popping of pine resin.*

Stephen J. Krasemann

*The same leaves over and over again!*
*They fall from giving shade above*
*To make one texture of faded brown*
*And fit the earth like a leather glove.*

*Robert Frost*

*. . . there appears to be no good reason for a tree to take on scarlet, gold or wine. A brilliant flower can attract the pollinating insect or bird it needs for the plant's reproduction, but a brilliant leaf attracts only the gaze of its admirer.*

Ron Lanner

*I rejoice that there are owls. Let them do the idiotic and maniacal hooting for men. It is a sound admirably suited to swamps and twilight woods which no day illustrates . . .*
*They represent the stark twilight and unsatisfied thoughts which we all have.*

Henry David Thoreau

*The woods were made for the hunter of dreams,*
*The brooks for the fishers of song.*

Sam Walter Foss

*To be able to follow unfamiliar watercourses days, weeks and months, to contend with wind and wave, to sleep in the open under pines or beside leaping water, to view sun and shadow on the changing scene of woodland, rock and water, to hobnob with the wild creatures . . . all this is the cherished dream of every true American.*

Ernest C. Oberholtzer

*The bull frogs trump to usher in the night, and the note of the whippoorwill is borne on the rippling wind from over the water. Sympathy with the fluttering alder and poplar leaves almost takes away my breath; yet, like the lake, my serenity is rippled but not ruffled.*

Henry David Thoreau

*Our ability to perceive quality in nature
   begins, as in art, with the pretty. It expands
through successive stages of the beautiful to
   values as yet uncaptured by language.*

Aldo Leopold

*A* lake is the landscape's most beautiful and expressive feature. It is earth's eye; looking into which the beholder measures the depth of his own nature.

Henry David Thoreau

*I* was in a twilight sleep in our rented
cabin on a northern Minnesota lake.
The night's memory of a loon's eerie
cries still reverberated in my
consciousness that early morning . . .

Philip Sutton Chard

*The wolf is a symbol of freedom and wide open space. Many things draw me to it: its tenacity in surviving against all odds; its unique form of government; its skill as a hunter.*

Stephen J. Krasemann

Forests are made for weary men,
    That they might find their souls again;
And little leaves are hung on trees,
    To whisper of old memories . . .

        Mary Carolyn Davies

*Nature, like a kind and smiling mother, lends herself to our dreams and cherishes our fancies.*

Victor Hugo

*What is art? Nature concentrated.*
Balzac

*Again let us dream where the land lies sunny*
*And live, like the bees, on our hearts' old honey,*
*Away from the world that slaves for money—*
*Come journey the way with me.*

*Madison Cawein*

*The snowdrop and primrose our woodlands adorn,*
*And violets bathe in the wet o' the morn.*

Burns